He Is Still The Miracle Worker

HE IS STILL THE
MIRACLE WORKER

Frank Acosta

XULON PRESS

Xulon Press
2301 Lucien Way #415
Maitland, FL 32751
407.339.4217
www.xulonpress.com

Paperback ISBN-13: 978-1-6628-4399-0
Ebook ISBN-13: 978-1-6628-4400-3

Contents

Preface

In the Holy Bible, Jesus told the man from whom He had cast out the legion of demons, "to go home and tell his friends, and tell them what great things the Lord hath done for thee, and hath had compassion on thee." (Mk. 5:19)

That is the main reason why I've decided to write this book. To tell people what great things He has done in our lives. Every day miracles happen somewhere on our planet. What exactly is a miracle? Google tells me, "a surprising and welcome event that is not explicable by nature or scientific laws and is therefore consider to be the work of a divine agency."

Whether people believe in miracles or not, that's their choice, but I believe in miracles because I'm a witness to a great number of them. The Holy Bible is full of miracles, from Genesis to Revelation. The Bible says Jesus did many miracles, and I believe in all of them, from turning the water to wine (John chapter 2) to His resurrection (John chapter 20). The main miracle I've received was the born again experience in my life, the day I gave my life to the Lord Jesus Christ. If you are not born again , you may not know what I'm talking about . A true believer in God knows and understands what I'm talking about.

So, in this book I want to share with you some of these supernatural events which I've witnessed in my short life time . I say "short" because our lives on Earth are in reality short. My prayer is that whosoever reads this book will have a closer walk with God, and those who don't know the Lord will feel the need to know the Lord in a personal way. For I know *He is the Miracle Worker*.

CHAPTER I

LIVING IN CRYSTAL CITY, TEXAS

My life began on June 6, 1954, when I was born in Crystal City, Texas, as Francisco Castillo Acosta.

Crystal City is located ninety-two miles Southwest of San Antonio, Texas, and thirty-five miles from the Mexico border, and as of 1990 had a 98 percent Mexican -American population . This town is best known as "the Spinach Capital of the World ," and has a statue of Popeye in front of City Hall. The name of the town comes from the artesian clear water in the area.

Back then, our family consisted of my father, Leonardo, mother, Catarina, my two older brothers, Juan (John), Jesus (Jesse) and me. Years later, Mother told me she had a daughter, born after Juan, who had passed away around two years young.

Everyone called me Panchi , a more loving name for Pancho . Mom never called me Panchi . She either called me Pancho or Frankie, and it was Pancho when she was mad.

My dad was hardly around, because he was, as many men in town were, a migrant worker, gone away from home for months, and even years. In fact, in the four year s I lived in Crystal City, I hardly remember him being around. I think Mom left him, when I was four years young, because his life and priorities were work first, then being with his drinking buddies, and family last.

I have fond memories of the time we lived in Crystal City. We lived in an old house with mesquite trees close by. The street where we lived was not paved. Many streets weren't paved in the 1950 s . Today is different, because now the streets are paved. Across the street lived a family who were close friends of ours. Their family consisted of the father, mother and their three children. The father was also a migrant worker and hardly around. The mother was Mom's best friend. Many times, they went shopping together, and their children were our close friends, too. The two boys were usually hanging around my brothers. They had a younger sister my age. She and I were always playing together. We were not old enough to attend school and it seemed like almost every day she came over to our house or I would go to her house to play. I can't remember their names because this was about sixty years ago. I just remember her as Elia, which I called her because I couldn't pronounce her name.

Many years later, in the early 1990 s, Mom and I went to Crystal City, because I wanted to see if it was the way I remembered it back when I was a boy. When we got there, I asked around to see if we could find Mom's friend, and we did. About thirty-five years had gone by since we had seen her. She was happy to see us and invited us inside, and since it was already evening, she invited us to spend the night there. Since she and Mom had a lot to talk about, she told me which room to sleep in. Once in the room, I was looking at the pictures on the wall. I think this room was my friend's Elia's room, for there were pictures of a young girl, and another one of a young woman in her high school graduation attire, and she was very beautiful. I felt sad we didn't stay in town and grow up there, so that I and Elia could possibly have gotten to know each other better. But it seems we had different destinies. For many days, this girl in the pictures was on my mind. I don't know why our destinies made us go our separate ways, but if God had different plans for us, I think He did so to lead us into a personal relationship with Him . I'm so glad He did.

I can say Crystal City was and is like any typical American town, except almost everyone spoke Spanish. All the children passed their time playing marbles and with toys such as yoyo s and top s, which we called a "tronco ." The main attraction on the weekends was while parents went shopping, we kids went to the movie theaters. In town were two main theaters, one

3

to show Mexican movies and the other to show Anglo movies. We went to watch Mexican movies. As a child, I remember movies about charros . These were Mexican singing cowboys , dressed up in their attire of matching pants and jackets with a sombrero , a big round hat, and guns at their waists. Their songs and the music were very professional and attracted the beautiful women. Some of our heroes we liked to see were Cantiflas , Piporro , Luis Aguilar , and Pedro Infante .

So, on Saturdays, my two brothers and I and the boys across the street would get together and walk downtown to a movie. To get there we took a short cut where we had to walk through an area with mesquite trees. There were cactus plants there, but we went through a trail . I remember one late evening. We were walking back home through this area and the movie we had watched was about a monster.

As we walked, I yelled, "The monster is following us ." I started running and everyone did too. But as I came to a curve, I slipped and fell in a patch of cactus plants. As I was crying, the boys came and pulled me out from the cactus and pulled out all the thorns from my body.

Mom's friend across the street had a shower room close to their house, and one time, some kids and I were taking a shower and making a lot of noise. Again, as usual, I was trying to scare the kids .

I climbed into the window and yelled, " The kukuo (the boogeyman) is coming!" As I said that, my hands slipped from the window and landed on a glass bowl. The bowl broke and cut my buttocks really bad. Mom's friend wrapped a towel around me. Mom came to take me to the doctor, who sewed me up to close the wounds. I guessed it doesn't pay to lie and be mischievous. I was reaping what I sowed.

According to Galatians 6:7, 8, "…For he that sows to his flesh shall of the flesh reap corruption, but he that sows to the Spirit shall of the Spirit reap life everlasting."

In the middle of all these, I was receiving my just payment for disobeying God. Today, we see all the bad things happening in the world, like wars, hunger, tragedies, murders, even nature bringing destruction upon man, etc. All these are the result of man's rebellion against God by siding with the devil, to bring all type of suffering to God's creation. Romans 2:8-11 says, "But unto them who are contentious, and do not obey the truth, but obey unrighteousness, indignation, wrath, tribulation and anguish, upon every soul of man that doeth evil, of the Jew first, and also of the Greek (Gentile), but glory, honor, and peace to every man that worked good, to the Jew first, and also to the Greek . For there is no respect of persons with God."

My older brother, Juan, was the meanest of the three of us. One time, Mom bought him a BB gun rifle and he told me and Jesse to run back and forth, while he shot us with his BB gun rifle. He managed to hit us and it hurt. Another time, Mom bought Juan a pair of cowboy boots and he really hated them. That day he took them and threw them in the outhouse. When Mom found out, she made him take them out. He did get them out, but I'm not saying how he did it.

By 1958, our family was about to start a new chapter in our lives. Mom had already met Silvestre Rivera, who was to become our stepfather. From this union, two more brothers were added to the family. They were Rodolfo (Rudy), born in 1959, in Wisconsin, while our parents were doing the cucumber harvest, and Roberto (Robert), born in Grand Forks, North Dakota. Sugar beets, potatoes and wheat were the main crops there.

One summer, our parents and two older brothers worked thinning sugar beets in South Dakota. We lived on a farm where there were hogs, chickens and cattle. Here is where I got my first taste of milk that came straight from the cow.

CHAPTER II

MOVING TO CLINTON

The family went on migrant labor from 1958 through 1965, traveling from Texas to the states up north. In Texas we lived in Wichita Falls, Dodson, Munday, and Goree, before we bought a house in Clinton, Oklahoma, on 512 North 2nd Street, next to the Salvation Army building. This was to be our home base, coming back from Minnesota in the winter.

This was the same year I started school at Washington Elementary School, located on North 13th Street and Nowahy Avenue. I was eleven years young at the time. Some of my fellow students were Barbara Driscoll, Sally Macmillan, Randy Rau, Stanley Wilson, Steve Hoffman, David Schoonmaker, and Ray White. Also the following, now deceased : Mike Rehder, Barry Cobb and Brad Quinn. I met Brad's father many years later, when I started working in the U.S. Post Office, in 1981 . He was a clerk there.

For some reason, coming to Clinton was a good choice, for we made many friends. It seemed like the people there opened their arms to us. Across the street from our house lived an older couple, whose last name was Crom. They bec ame real good friends of ours. The many times we spent working in Minnesota, they looked after our house. If they saw something or someone suspicious around our house, he or she came out and told them to get away.

I made good friends around the block. There was a native boy named Sammy Lee and a boy named Scott Rutherford, whose father was Jay C. Rutherford. Mr. Rutherford, back then, was a mailman . I also met him again in 1981, when I went to work at the U.S. Post Office as a clerk-mail-carrier . Scott would usually come over to play at our house. In fact, he was almost part of the family. Sometimes, Mom would invite him to eat with us, and he probably tasted home-made Mexican food for the first time at our house. He sometimes stayed longer than usual, and his sister, Kim, came over to tell him it was time to go home. Now, Kim would come dressed in her brown Girl Scout uniform . I had a crush on her, but I was shy around girls. One day, Mr. Rutherford got home from work, and still in his mailman's uniform, came over to tell Scott to go home. As I looked through the window, Scott's dad removed his belt and hit Scott on his rear and he jumped up, crying, rubbing his bottom.

I got to see Mr. Quinn and Mr. Rutherford retire from work around the middle of the 1980 s. These two men were veterans of World War II. I retired from the Postal Service on December 31, 2020, and as far as I know, Mr. Rutherford is alive and living in the town of Cordell. In 1972, we bought a house on South 10th Street, and Mr. Rutherford was our mailman until he retired from work.

Years later, when Scott was in the Air Force, he lived in the southeast part of the country, where he married and raised a family. Years later, he worked driving a semi-truck and moved back to Oklahoma.

I also have a brother and sister from my stepdad's previous marriage, still living in San Antonio, Texas : Silvestre Rivera, Jr., and Consuelo "Chelo" Napoles . I also have a brother-in-law, Sgt. Luis Penida, retired, who was married to my late sister, Josefina, who is with the Lord.

CHAPTER III

THE GROUND PREPARED FOR THE SEED

In St. Matthew 13:8, Jesus talks about the sower who went to plant the seed : "But other seeds fell into good ground, and brought forth fruit, some an hundred-fold, some sixtyfold, and some thirtyfold." Here Jesus uses the parable of the sower who went out to plant the seed, verses 3-9. And in verses 18-23, He explains the parable to His disciples. You see, the sower here is those who speak the Word of God, the seed is the Word of God, and the ground is the heart of the hearer. If the farmer does not prepare the ground before he plants the seed, the ground will not yield a good crop. But if he works the field before he plants the seed, it will yield a good crop. God in His great wisdom made it possible for my family and me to hear His Word and He did at the right moment because the "ground was ready to receive the seed."

My family and I were migrant workers, and we went to work in the fields in Minnesota till 1979 . We traveled from Clinton, Oklahoma, to Climax, Minnesota, from early May till late October every year. My family was made up of my stepdad, mother and four brothers. All five of us siblings had to work in the fields when we were old enough, around sixteen years of age. The main crops we helped the farmer with were sugar beets, potatoes and wheat. We lived in a farm close to where the farmer lived. His name was Joe Quirk and he lived with his wife, two daughters and a son. Mr. Quirk came from an Irish background. Joe, whose first name was Edward, had a worker everyone called Eddie.

My family came from a Catholic background, and when we didn't work on Saturday, we would attend Mass on Sundays. All except my stepdad, who stayed home. I never knew if he was Catholic or not.

I feel blessed that God worked in our lives in a miraculous way. In this book I will name some of the miracles God did in our lives. I am a witness to what the Lord has done in our lives. In Hebrews 13:8, it says, "Jesus Christ is the same yesterday, today and forever." After Mother came to the Lord, I remember her writing in a notebook the miracles God did in her life. Even though her notebooks either got lost or misplaced, I still remember what God did in her life.

The purpose of this book is not to give credit to man, but to God , because He alone deserves all the credit and glory. All the people in the Bible who received a miracle from God gave glory to God. Even before my family was saved, God was already working in our lives in marvelous ways.

As I said, before growing up in a migrant family, as a young child, I remember my mother often getting sick. She suffered from stomach ulcers. During the time when we didn't have a town to settle in yet , there were times I thought we were going to lose her, because I saw her in pain often. When we arrived in Clinton, Oklahoma, my stepdad took her to the Clinton Hospital, back when the hospital was located on South 8th Street.

Many years later, while she was in the hospital, suffering with ulcers, she called upon God to heal her. Now, I don't know what words she said, but God did hear her prayer and healed her of her suffering. I don't know if she asked God to save her or not, but her healing gave her faith to believe in Jesus as her personal Savior, one day.

I also remember, when I was about twenty years old, we drove trucks in Minnesota during harvest season, and worked many hours driving. We would haul sugar beets from the fields to the factory and returned to the field to repeat the process. The most I worked, one day, was eighteen hours. It was getting close to October, and the farmers knew that once the snow started falling, it might not stop, resulting in the loss of their crop. We drove tandem-trucks, with eight wheels in the back.

The loads we carried were between 25,000 to 31,000 pounds. There were times I fell asleep while driving, and I don't know how long I drove, asleep. It could have been a few seconds. I woke up because my leg jumped up while I was still driving, and this scared me. I opened the window a little bit and turned the heater down to keep me from falling asleep again. My brother Jesse told me one day that the same thing happened to him some times. You can say it was luck, but I believe God sent an angel to move our legs. The good Lord had good plans for my brothers and me, for one day we would be serving the Lord.

Another time, coming back to Oklahoma after harvest in Minnesota, my stepdad was driving our fairly new GMC truck. He had to pull over and stop because the truck started making a lot of noise in the back, around the tires. He got off the truck to check if he could find out what the problem was, but didn't see anything out of the ordinary, so he got back in the truck, drank some coffee, and drove off. Now, I don't know what made that noise, but I believe God intervenes in our lives, to keep us from having a bad accident. The Bible says in Psalm 34:7, "The angel of the Lord encampeth round about those who fear Him, and delivereth them." (NSRB) In this book, I will mention the many times God protected me and my family from being involved in bad accidents.

Chapter IV

OUR PARENTS' ENCOUNTER WITH GOD

There were times our parents went to Texas to visit family, and Robert, being the youngest, went with them. During one of these occasions, while in Texas, my stepdad started having chest pains. He told mother it was better if they went back to Oklahoma. So, they did. Mom drove back, and once they arrived in Clinton, she drove straight to the Catholic church and parked in the front of the church. She told Robert to go find the priest and ask him if he could come outside and pray for Dad.

To Mom's surprise, Robert came back, but the priest was not with him. Mother asked Robert where the priest was and he said the priest told him he was busy and couldn't come out to pray.

Then my dad said, "I told you not to bring me here." So, they went home.

Another time, my stepsister came from San Antonio to visit. Her name was Josephine and she was my step-dad's daughter from a previous marriage. Josephine and her husband, Sgt. Luis Pineda, retired from the Army, had recently been saved in a church in San Antonio .

What happened next was the most wonderful thing, which changed our lives forever. On this particular day, Josephine, my dad and mom were home talking. Dad started having those chest pains and Josephine said, "I'm going to call the priest to come pray for you."

Dad said, "Don't bother, he won't come."

So, she picked up the phone and asked the priest if he would come and pray for Dad because he wasn't feeling well. And again, the priest told my sister he was busy and couldn't come.

My sister told him, " How is it you're ready to accept my dad's offering he sent you by mail ?"

She hung up the phone and went through the Yellow Pages and found an Assembly of God minister and called to ask if he would come pray for Dad. He said yes and came over and prayed for Dad, and Dad got better. My sister explained to the minister how the priest refused to come and pray for Dad. The minister invited my parents to his church and they started attending there.

Now, before you accuse me of a "hate crime ," I don't hate Catholics, because we used to be Catholics. I think some Catholics are sincere and they're truly trying to serve God, but it's like Jesus said, "Verily,

verily, I say unto thee, except a man be born again, he cannot see the Kingdom of God." (Jn. 3:3) Without the born again birth, you will never understand or "see" the Kingdom of God.

My parents started attending the Assembly of God church, and the minister noticed while he was preaching, Dad was interpreting for Mom what the minister was saying, because she didn't understand English. And one day the minister suggested to Dad it would be good if my parents attended a Spanish-speaking church located on Frisco Avenue, so Mom could understand without Dad having to interpret the sermon. However, my parents were still welcome to come visit his church any time. That was how my parents started attending this Spanish Assembly of God church on South 4th Street and Frisco Avenue. The people having services there were renting the building, which used to be a bank in the old days. This building is no long there. It's a vacant lot.

One day, Mother told us boys that we all were going to attend this church, and I remember thinking , *I'm a Catholic, will always be a Catholic and will die a Catholic*. I never thought God had other plans for me. I remember the first time we went to church there. People were singing, clapping their hands, and were really happy . The atmosphere felt really nice and I liked it. Now I know God brought us to this church because He was about to do something great in our lives.

CHAPTER V

HOW MY BROTHERS AND I CAME TO GOD

I n the following pages, I'm going to tell you how my brothers and I came to God. In Acts 16:31, it says, "Believe on the Lord Jesus Christ, and thou shalt be saved, and thy house." (NSRB) Now it doesn't say, "do good works, or believe in your own religion." It says, "Believe on the Lord **Jesus Christ**." Why is it so hard for people to understand that?

You might say, "I thought your book was about miracles and not about how you got saved." Well, the salvation of one's soul is a big miracle in itself, because the moment you believe on the Lord Jesus with your heart and confess Him, and believe God raised Him from the dead, you shall be saved. (Rom. 10:9, 10) That means the moment you say that prayer and believe it in your heart (faith), you are saved. Ephesians 2:8, 9 reads, "For by grace are ye saved through faith; and that not of yourselves, it is the gift of God—not of works lest any man should boast." (NSRB) What I'm telling you, folks, is real and not a figment of my imagination.

I want to go back in time, before I was a Christian, to say how God already had His hand on me to be part of His Kingdom

I remember one time, when I was about fifteen years old, my two younger brothers, Rudy and Robert and I and another boy, a friend of the family, were going down a gravel road in a 1955 Chevrolet . I was driving, going about 55 mph and playing with the steering wheel and everyone was laughing. I lost control of the car and it overturned, landing in the ditch with the wheels pointing up. Now, it was no laughing matter. I was so scared. I rushed to see if anyone was hurt and thank God everyone was fine. It didn't go well with my dad after I told him that I had wrecked the car. This car was used by the family to go work in the fields of Minnesota.

There was a time when I was about twenty-three years old, my brothers, Rudy and Robert and I were going back home in Jesse's car. I was driving. Jesse was arrested for DWI and put in jail. It was at night and really cold outside. As I approached a low spot on the road, I lost control of the car, because there was ice on the road. We went in the ditch and came out and landed in a field that was recently plowed. I told my brothers to get out and push the car while I drove the car, which they did, to get the out of the field. I thank

God to this day, because when I was driving, if the car would have veered to the right of the road, where there was a deep gorge, I believe we wouldn't be alive today . God saved us.

The next time I came close to dying in a car accident was around 1977. Back then, I had a 1970 Barracuda, yellow, with a black vinyl top. It had to be on Saturday evening when I was "dragging" on the main street with two of my friends. Jesse was also dragging main with his girlfriend, Ranae. My brother stopped me and told me to take the car home and park it, because he knew I was drinking. He said I could have an accident in my car and could die.

I told him, " Everybody dies sooner or later ." The beer was already taking effect on me. I didn't listen to him, That night, my friends and I drank beer and hard liquor and took pills. To this day, I don't know what they were.

That night, coming back to Clinton on Highway 183, in front of the Veteran's Center, my car veered to the left and went into the ditch and hit a sign that said, Keep Right . That was it, I had wrecked my car. But it was like I was dreaming. It didn't seem like it was happening in real life. A man in his car stopped and asked if we needed a ride to town. My friends said yes, but I stayed in the car. It didn't take long before the police arrived and took me out of the car and straight to jail.

The next day, my dad went to the police station, paid the fine and took me home.

Later in the day, my dad took me to where the car was to see if it could be fixed, but it was a total loss. The front center was all smashed in and the man there kept asking my dad if I was okay, because the steering wheel was bent down. Thank You, Jesus for saving me and those with me from death in these car wrecks .

One of the young men in the last car wreck with me was Gilbert Rogue. Later, I found out he moved to Chicago, and he too got saved. The other young man was from Texas and had been visiting family in Clinton. Well, he went back to Texas and I don't know what became of him.

Once again, someone might say it was a coincidence or pure luck . You can say whatever you want, but I said what I believe and believe what I said.

There was a time in Minnesota when my brother and a friend and I went swimming in a lake near our house. While in the lake, I went under the water and took in water. In desperation, I went up and managed to move to where it was safer and stayed there the rest of the day.

1978 was the turning point in my life, for in April of that year my dad passed away from pneumonia . I, being the oldest boy at home, had to take on responsibility as the man of the house. My two older brothers had married and now our family living at home was me, my mom and my two younger brothers, Rudy and Robert. These two brothers had the last names of Rivera, because of they came from Mom's second marriage to my stepdad, Silvestre.

The next day after Dad died, I called Joe Quirk, the farmer we worked for in Minnesota, to tell him the sad news. He asked me if we were still going to Minnesota to work, and I told him yes.

We left for Minnesota around the first week of May. John and Jesse, along with their wives, also went in their own cars. Now, before we arrived at the farm, one of us went up ahead to go in the house and remove anything that belonged to Dad, so Mom would not see them and become sad . But after we arrived, Mom hurried and went in the house and saw my dad's hat hanging on the wall and she started crying. All of us got around her and managed to comfort her.

Not long after we returned to the farm, it was the. middle of the night and everyone was asleep, when the car outside started honking. Everyone woke up to find the house full of black smoke. So, we opened all the windows, and the one door of the house to let the smoke out. Then, we went outside to check who honked the horn on the car, but no one was in it. So how did the horn go off? I believe God had something to do with it, because who knows what would have happened if we didn't wake up ? Thank God for sending the angel to honk the horn to wake us up.

So many things the Lord has done in our lives. Why not serve Him and thank Him every day?

As a young man, I used to have a nose bleed problem. This problem started when I was around eight years old, and I had a nose bleed almost every day. One day my parents heard of a man who prayed for the sick. The people got healed and he charged whatever they could pay him. So, my parents decided to take me to him so he would pray for me. The man was German-American. When I was there, the man laid hands on me and prayed for me. I don't remember the words he said, but I did get better. Occasionally I still had a nose bleed, but eventually it stopped. Praise God! I had had this problem for about five or six years.

Going forward to the summer of 1978, we were thinning sugar beets in a field when a woman stopped to invite us to church on Sunday. Mom said yes, we would go. The church was in a small town called Fisher, Minnesota, and they were having evangelical services in Spanish. The minister finished the sermon and invited people forward who wanted to get saved. I went to the altar and knelt down to receive the Lord Jesus as my personal Savior. This time, my name was written down in the Book of Life and I became a citizen in the Kingdom of God, or as we sometimes say, a citizen of Heaven. (Rev. 3:5) I was about to begin a life-changing experience. (Jn. 3:3) I was twenty-four years old.

In 1980, my brother Rudy and I, along with Jose Castro, were baptized at Foss Lake by Rev. Clemente Maldonado, Jr.

Rudy got saved in 1977, as a result of God healing him of a pain he suffered in his arm. He told me he prayed to God to heal him from that pain and the Lord answered and that gave him faith to believe.

Next to be saved was my older brother, John, who was more rebellious than the rest of us boys. One time, as a young man, he was drinking in his car and he got stopped by a sheriff outside of town. The sheriff, who also was drinking, was kind of out of line and began hitting John with his baton . That made John angry, and he started fighting and hitting the sheriff. John got arrested and was taken to the Custer County Jail and put in solitary. The day of his court trial, the sheriff didn't show up, so John's case was dismissed. As time went on, John had minor run-ins with the law, but mostly for DWI. John liked the car model, Javelin, and he owned two on different occasions, but he wrecked both while drinking and driving.

As time went on, John met and married a young woman from Hobart, Oklahoma, about forty miles from Clinton. Her name was Elizabeth and she was the daughter of the Rev. Ernesto Chapa, a Pentecostal minister, who was the pastor of a Spanish church in Hobart. John would later say that he would go to this church while drinking and would sit on the back bench with his friend. Now Elizabeth's (or Beth, as I called her) parents didn't approve of her dating a man who was drinking most of the time. But Beth continued dating him, and in February 1974, they married. A year or two later, while living in Clinton, they had a son, John, Jr.

When John told Joe Quirk, the farmer in Minnesota, that he got married, Joe put a mobile home trailer close to the house where we lived while working there. Beth was a hard-working young woman. She helped John thin sugar beets in the field, and the rows in some fields were half a mile long. This was in the summer and the weather there reached 100 degrees Fahrenheit on some days.

Now John was not a Christian yet, nor was Beth, even though she was a minister's daughter, which was not unusual. There were times they got into arguments. Sometimes, my younger brother, Robert, would stay with them and would tell Mom about the arguing. One of those night when they were arguing, John went and picked up a loaded .22 rifle, pointed it at Beth, and pulled the trigger, but the rifle didn't fire, Thank God it didn't go off, because God had other plans for this couple.

The next day, Beth went to our house and called her parents to tell them she didn't want to be with John any-more, and wanted to go back home to live with them. Her parents' advice was not what she wanted to hear. They told her no, because she knew how John was before she married him. She was told to fight for her marriage, and they would pray for both her and John. Over half of all marriages wind up in divorce because couples want the easy way out. When couples get married, they make a solemn vow to stay together, through health and sickness, through riches or poverty, through good or bad times. Despite that, they divorce and break that vow, which they made not to the minister, but to God. Beth obeyed her parents, and at the time of writing this book, they've been married for almost forty-six years.

Before John married, one day after work, some friends of his came to the farm where we were working, thinning sugar beets, to pick him up to go drinking . John told them another time, because he had gotten off work and was tired. This happened in 1970 . The young man driving t his new '70 model Plymouth GTX 440 HP was named Richard , and three other young men were with him. We knew these three young men because they had worked with us thinning sugar beets. That night, they wrecked the car. Three of them died and one survived only because he was thrown out the back window and landed in the ditch . He was in the hospital for many days. His name was "Beto" Gonzales . One of the three who died in the wreck was his eighteen-year-old brother.

The last time I saw Beto was in a fair in town, and he was so drunk that his friends had to hold him up. The sad part was that Richard had bought that new car with insurance money he collected after his father died in an accident while driving a semi-truck . I think God helped my brother choose not to go with those four boys, and saved him from the horrible accident.

John said one time before that accident, he was with Richard in the same car, headed to a Mexican dance in another town, and going down the highway at 130 mph. Richard missed a curve and went into the ditch, but managed to put the car back on the road. There were six young men in the car.

You know, people never think about death . They don't wake up in the morning and say, "Today is the day I'm going to die." But think how many times death hits close to home or comes knocking at our doors. That's why it's so important people get right with God. 2 Timothy 4:1 says, "I charge thee, therefore, before God, and the Lord Jesus Christ, who should judge the living and the dead at His appearing and His Kingdom." In short, to explain in simple terms, if you're living for Jesus, you'll be rewarded with eternal life in Heaven, but if you stand before God as a "sinner ," you'll be condemned forever. (J n. 3:16)

Now, my brother John was not all bad. He had a good side, too. If you treated him nice, he treated you nice too, but if you treated him bad, he would let you know you shouldn't have. I remember Mom saying, before she and dad were Christians, when they would visit family in San Antonio, and they would go and visit this woman who sold them herbs and "medicines" to help people change, to behave better. But Mom would say, instead of getting better when he took the "medicine," John got worse.

I thank God for the many doctors out there who are helping people with physical illness, but when it comes to "disorder behavior," that has to do with the spirits and the minds of people. The problem is spiritual, and it needs to be dealt with spiritually. God is the doctor who can not only heal the physical, but the mind and the spirit as well. Jesus said in Luke 4:18, He not only came to preach the gospel, but also to heal the brokenhearted, to preach deliverance to the captives, and recovering of sight to the blind, to set at liberty those are bruised , so the remedy is in the preaching and accepting of the Word of the Living God. Jesus is the remedy to all of man's problems, whatever they may be.

Many people blame God for all the problems in the world, but the problem is man siding with Satan to do evil things . According to John 10:10, Satan came to rob, to kill and to destroy , but Jesus came to give us life in abundance.

Next, I want to tell how John came to know Jesus Christ as his personal Savior.

Around 1976, Jesse married his girlfriend, Renae Risinger, in Clinton. That year, when we loaded up the truck and cars and headed for Minnesota to do farm labor , Jesse and Renae moved into John and Beth's mobile home, while John, Beth, and John Jr. were in another one.

John was hired by another farmer, about eight miles from where we were, and about half a mile from Fisher, the small town where I had gotten saved.

One day, John was plowing a field in a big four-wheel tractor that had a radio and air conditioning in it. John would later tell us, on that day he had the radio on and changed to a Christian station . A singer who was Hawaiian happened to be singing, and that song touched my brother. He felt the conviction of the Holy Spirit come upon him. He stopped the tractor, got off, kneeled on the ground and asked God to forgive all his sins. From that moment forward, he was a different man. He said a whirlwind came and surrounded him and moved on . He had plans that day to go home after work and then go to the bar in town and have a few beers, but his plans never happened because the Lord saved him.

As time went by, Beth saw the change God had made in John, and she, too, accepted Jesus as her personal Savior. The farmer John worked for was Sheldon Jorgensen.

Next to come into the Kingdom of God was Jesse. Like John, he was also a weekend drinker. Now Jesse was the kind of guy who would drink beer on a Friday night, go home around two or three in the morning, and the next day would get up early, like 7:00 am to go to work. He was a hard-working man. Once , he and John competed to see who would thin more sugar beet rows in one day. Jesse won.

1979 was the last time we made the long trip to Minnesota as migrant workers. By this time, Dad had gone on to be with the Lord. Mom, Beth, Rudy and I were Christians. Mom would invite Jesse to church, but he said he was already going to the Catholic church.

As time went on, Jesse and Renae had three boys and a girl. When they were all grown up, Jesse was a welder with a welding rig and worked in the oil fields.

One day, Jesse and Renae separated, and Mom again invited Jesse to church. This time he went to the Pentecostal church we attended, and it didn't take long for him to accept the Lord as his personal Savior after hearing the gospel. Jesse would later testify how God had saved him from having serious accidents at work. Now, I never welded, especially on oil pipelines or oil field equipment, but I know how dangerous this job is. There were times Jesse had to go up the oil rig and hold on to the railing with one hand and do the welding with the other hand. He said one time he was doing a welding job inside a large tank and the sparks from the welding landed on some oil in the tank and started a fire. When he saw the fire, he dropped everything and got out of the tank and didn't get burned.

Mother went on to be with the Lord in 2014, and Jesse went around 2016. During his funeral service, somebody said, "In the years I've known Jesse, I never heard him say a cuss word ." Then it dawned on me, in all my life, even when we were growing up , I, too, didn't hear him say a cuss word. That's unusual, because I, as a child and teenager, cursed a lot. Thank God that stopped when I came to the Lord.

CHAPTER VI

HEALING MIRACLES

Next, I want to tell about some miracles of healing I've seen in my life time. I remember when my mother and I were living in our house, all my brothers had married and had moved out. Mother was cooking and was about to go down the basement to get a bigger bowl. Well, at that moment she slipped, went down, and hit her lower back on the wooden steps. I called someone for help and managed to get her to her room, but the fall had done great damage to her lower back. After we took her to her doctor, he said Mom had cracked her lower back bone. At the moment, there wasn't a whole lot the doctor could do, except give her pain pills and put a brace around her back.

In the following days, Mom was having excruciating pain and needed help to get around. It hurt me to see her in that condition. On one trip to the doctor, she was told to stay home and not to go out of the house .

She told the doctor she wanted to go to church, but the doctor said no.

One day, a black minister, who had the gift of healing, was going to be in town at Pop Hick's Restaurant in the back guest room, which was large enough to have a service. When Mom heard of it, she said she wanted to go . I said it was better if she didn't, because of her condition. When the day of the service came, John and Beth took her, and thank God they did, because He was about to do a miracle in her life.

This was in the winter, and the day was cold and it had snowed . I didn't go, but Mom would later say the place was packed with people. During the service, while the minister was preaching, the Holy Spirit gave him a word of knowledge. He said someone in the service was in great pain, and the Lord was going to heal that person. Mom looked around to see if anyone would stand up . When she didn't see anyone get up, she raised her hand. After the minister knew what was wrong with her, he prayed for her and said the Lord had healed her.

After the service, everyone went home, but Mom was still in pain. This happened in the early 80 s. That night, I told Mom I was going to sleep in the kitchen, which was next to her bedroom, so I could help her if she needed to get up. She said it was okay, I could sleep in my room, and if she needed help she would call out to me. I could just leave the door to my room open, so I could hear her.

Well, I slept all night, and in the morning, around 6 a.m., I woke up and saw the kitchen light on and it smelled like someone was cooking in the kitchen. I thought, *Who can it be ? It's just me and Mom at home.* So, I got up to go check, and to my surprise, Mom was cooking breakfast for me.

I said, "Mom, what are you doing?"

She said, "Son, go wash up and come sit down, because I have something wonderful to tell you."

She told me , around 2 a.m., her back was hurting really bad. She was calling out to God to help her with the pain, and she heard a voice say, "You can't get up because you're in great pain." Then she heard the voice say , " Get up and pray for Alejandro." And then a second voice spoke , saying the same thing. On the third time, the first voice spoke with authority. Immediately, Mom jumped up from her bed and put her feet on the floor lightly to see if there was any pain, and there was no pain. Then she went to the side of the door and rubbed her back against it, and again, no pain. Now she knew the Lord had healed her, so she started praising God and thanking Him for her miracle.

Then she remembered what the Lord told her to pray for. She knelt beside her bed and said, "Lord, I don't know who this Alejandro is, but if he is in any danger, save him, Lord."

Praise God! I have to confess, when I started writing about this miracle, I burst out crying like a baby. But the tears were of joy.

The next time we had church, when it was time to give thanks for what God did, a sister stood up and said she was thanking God because her husband was working on the oil rig way up on top and slipped and almost went down, but managed to hold on to the railing and didn't fall to his death. Mom asked her what was her husband's name, and she said, "Alejandro." Mom stood up and said the Lord had told her to pray for this man on a particular day of the week and the sister said it was the same day her husband almost had his accident.

Now I want to tell of another miracle the Lord did on Mom. This one happened while we were having church service at Templo Maranatha, 201 Prairie Chief Ave. I remember Mom having pain in her neck, and she had to wear a brace on her neck to keep it from hurting so much. As usual, she didn't want to miss the church service. When it came to church services, Mom was stubborn and refused to stay home. Sometimes, I saw her having pain and when it was cold outside, I would say to her, "It is better if you stayed home," but she would reply, "Son, if I stay home, I be in pain and if I go to church, I be in pain, but if I go to church maybe the Lord will heal me." Now that's what I call faith.

In the Bible, we read about people who, just before they received a miracle from God, had to go through obstacles . Like the woman with the issue of blood, in Mark 5:25. What was her obstacle? She had spent all her money consulting physicians only to get worse. The other obstacle was a crowd of people, which made it almost impossible to reach Jesus. Then there was Zacchaeus who had heard of Jesus and wanted to see Him. What was his obstacle? When Jesus came to town, Zacchaeus, being a short man, couldn't see Him because of the crowd in front of him. So, he ran and climbed the sycamore tree and Jesus took notice of his faith, and salvation came to him and his household. (L k . 19)

Back when we were in church, Brother Guillermo "Willie" Flores was preaching on the theme of faith. Mom was sitting in the front with the chair against the wall, where she usually sat. During the service Brother Willie, as we called him, turned to Mom and said, " Sister Rivera, the Lord tells me He is going to heal you tonight."

So, Mom stood up and came to the front. As Brother Willie was praying for her, from the side of the pulpit, Mom took her brace off and started dancing in the Spirit, and praising God for healing her. Special moments like this are forever engraved in my mind, so I will never forget. I mean, it is like being in the presence of God when the Holy Spirit is doing something marvelous.

Now, back before Mom received the baptism of the Holy Spirit, my mom, my dad and my Aunt Simona Arreola were in a revival service in Del Rio, Texas.

37

During the service, people were going forward to be prayed for and some were being "slain" in the Spirit. Some were dancing in the Spirit. Mom was thinking , *When I receive the Holy Spirit, I don't want to make a lot of commotion.*

My mom and my aunt went forward to be prayed for. Mom would say later, she had her hands raised up, holding her purse in one hand and my aunt's purse on the other hand. All of a sudden, she started dancing in the Spirit, then was "slain" in the Spirit. One purse flew one way and the other one flew another way. That was a turning point in her life, and from that moment forward, she was radically changed.

The term "slain in the Spirit" is used in Pentecostal events, meaning when a person is slain in the Spirit, the Spirit of God comes upon them. His presence is so strong one can't remain standing up. For example, in Acts 9:4, Saul fell down when the bright light (Jesus) shone upon him. And in Revelation 1:17, "and when I saw Him, I fell at his feet as dead..." as recorded by the Apostle John.

CHAPTER VII

THE CALL INTO THE MINISTRY

A round 1981, Mother and I were called into the ministry to do God's work. We took study courses with the Assembly of God churches, finished, and were given credentials to do God's work. In 1982, we left this affiliation and started attending a Pentecostal church in Hobart, where Rev. Ernesto Chapa was pastor. For the next two years, Mom and I made a forty-mile trip to attend Sunday school and the evening service every Sunday.

Mom also attend ed the Wednesday service with John and Beth. Beth was the daughter of Rev. Chapa, and married my brother in 1974, the same year I grad-uated from Clinton High School. During the time we were in this church, Mom was the women's church president and I was the youth church president. We also helped in leading the service and preaching God's Word. The church was called Templo Sion. I have many wonderful memories from this church, as well as when we were with the Assembly of God church.

By the end of 1984, the Lord directed us to start a church in Clinton. Mom and I talked to Pastor Chapa to let him know our intentions, and he told us he would pray if it was God's will. About two weeks later, he gave us permission to start a mission in Clinton. Brother Chapa was also our Presbyter to North Texas and Oklahoma District churches, and the organization was The Unified Pentecostal Local Churches, Inc. We started having church services at our home and Rev. Chapa and his wife would come to lead in singing with his bass guitar. Later, we went looking for a place to rent and couldn't find one in Clinton, but found a place in Arapaho, a small town five miles north of Clinton. Mom was the pastor and I was the co-pastor. We were there for four years and God did many wonderful things in this place. We later rented a small church in Clinton, on Neptune Drive and were there for two years. From there we found another church to rent, on 201 Prairie Chief Avenue, and the church is still there.

Around 1988, Mom got sick and it was difficult for her to lead the church. By this time, Brother Chapa had closed the church in Hobart, and we invited him to come and be our pastor. There was another church in Texas that didn't have a pastor and had asked Brother Chapa to be their pastor. So, Brother Chapa prayed, and the Lord le d him to come to Clinton to be our pastor.

The mission in Arapaho was called The Spanish Mission, but later the name was changed to Templo Maranatha. Templo is Spanish for temple, and maranatha means, "Our Lord, Come ," taken from 1 Corinthians 16:22 (1960 KJV).

Before Mom got sick, she did the Lord's work for many years. Not just in Clinton, but in San Antonio, while visiting family there. She was invited to preach in some churches. I have a cousin in Austin , who back then would go to Mexico to do missionary work, along with her husband, Adolfo Cervantes. Her name is Noemi.

Before Mom went on these evangelical trips, she would pray and fast for a week or more and God would use her to do His work. You see, prayer and fasting are a sign of humbleness, letting God know we need Him to help us do His work more effectively.

Whenever Mom returned home, she would tell how God did miracles by people getting saved and healed when she prayed for them, praise God! On one occasion, she had just arrived from one of these trips and she was telling of all God had done. People had gotten saved and healed, and some were set free from demon possession and so forth. It was late at night and I had to go to bed. Before going to bed, I was praying, and I started speaking in tongues for the first time. I got up and went and told Mom. We both started thanking and praising the Lord, for Mom knew I had been seeking the baptism in the Holy Spirit for some time. This happened in 1982.

After my brothers married and moved out, Mom and I did the Lord's work for many years. During this time, Brother Willie came to our house to visit and asked me if I wanted to join him in his jail ministry, and I said yes. He and I would go to preach God's Word in the City and County jails, for about twenty years.

Me with mother and brothers. from- l-r, Robert,
Catarina, Rudy, Jesse, Silvestre Jr., John, and Frank

Catarina with daughters-in-law. from l-r--Terri,
Catarina(mom), Lorie, Elizabeth.

Frank delivering mail on his route in Clinton, Ok.

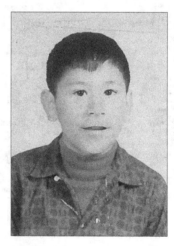

Frank's School picture in 1965.
In Washington Elementary School.

Elizabeth holding Jonathan (author's son) and John

Silvestre Rivera (stepdad) in East Grand Forks, Minnesota.

Jesse about 19 years old on his
Honda motorcycle in Minnesota.

Robert about 13 years old on Jesse's motorcycle.

Rudy, about 16 years old by his
Nova Chevrolet car. Minnesota

CHAPTER VIII

FAITH TESTED BY FIRE

In 1 Peter 1:7, it says, "that the trial of your faith, being much more precious than of gold that perisheth, though it be tried with fire, might be found unto praise and honor and glory at the appearing of Jesus Christ."

Around 1993, the Lord gave me a dream to prepare me for the great pain I was about to go through. When I had the dream, I didn't know what it meant, but later I did. In the dream I saw a giant black figure that was destroying cities, and I could see the smoke rising up to heaven behind him. Then he spoke to me and said, "Frank thinks I can't do anything to him, because he is trusting in his God." Then he started laughing out loud. Then he told me about all the cities he had destroyed, behind him. But I spoke to him with a loud voice, and pointing my finger at him, I said, "In the name of Jesus, I rebuke you." Then to my amazement, that thing began getting smaller until it was about the size of a Chihuahua . Tugging its tail in, it took off running like it had been kicked, making a weird sound.

After I woke up, I started searching in the Bible for any reference to the things I saw in my dream. I found it in Isaiah chapters 36 and 37, where something similar happened to King Hezekiah . The king of Assyria, who se name was Sennacherib, had sent his great army to destroy the fortified cities of Judah. A messenger had been sent to King Hezekiah, who was ruling from the fortified city of Jerusalem. The letter was read to the king's officials who were on the wall. Something in that letter was in my dream. That letter said King Hezekiah was trusting in his God to save them, but there was no god that saved the people in the cities Sennacherib had destroyed. This was similar to the giant figure who spoke to me in my dream. The message was relayed to King Hezekiah, who in turn called for the prophet Isaiah, then went to pray to God . (Is. 37:14-20) Then in verses 33-35, God said He was going to save Jerusalem from the King of Assyria and his army was not going to set their feet inside Jerusalem. In vrses 36-38, the angel of the Lord came by night and smote 185,000 of the Assyrians and King Sennacherib was murdered by his two sons as he worshiped his god in the temple.

Not long after I had that dream , I started having these terrible, unbearable headaches . I was diagnosed as having "cluster headaches ," which the doctor told me was like three migraine headaches hitting with full force. The next two years I suffered with these headaches and had them twice a year, last ing about two weeks each. Even the strongest medicine didn't take them away.

Then one day, Dr. Kirk Gastineau, who was a High School classmate of mine, gave me pills I was to take on a sliding scale for five days. The first day, five pills, decreasing until one the last day I took one pill, and thank God, no more headaches. Then, about 1999, I had another episode with this headache. We were in Fort Worth, Texas, visiting family at the time. By this time, I was married, and my wife and I had three chil-dren. The oldest was hers from a previous union, but I loved him and raised him as my own, and to this day he calls me Dad. Mom was also with us. I told Mom and my wife, Rosa, it was better if we headed back home because I felt the headache coming on. While we were driving back, Mom said, " Why not stop in a Quik shop and buy some Exedrin ?"

I did buy some, and lo and behold, after taking two pills the pain went away, and to this day, no more head-aches, praise God! Now, I don't know why God per-mitted this to happen to me. All I know is, maybe my faith was put to the test. All I know is, I'm still serving the Lord and that trial helped me have a closer relation-ship with God.

Back when Mom fell and God healed her from her pain , He told her even though she was going to be used by Him, she was also going to suffer for His name's sake.

I remember back in the early 60 s, Mom suffered from painful stomach ulcers and my dad was always taking care of her. Many times, Dad took her to the doctor and sometimes to the hospital. Around the mid 1960 s, she entered the Clinton Hospital, located on the 300 block of South Eighth Street. She would say later that she called unto God for help because she had a family to take care of. She asked the Lord to forgive her for her sins, and the Lord heard her prayer. She got better. While in the hospital bed, she looked out the window and began to appreciate nature; how beautiful were the green leaves on the trees, the flowers and the birds. It was like her eyes had been opened. She had experienced the born again miracle described in John 3:3,7, where Jesus told Nicodemus that he must be born again to enter into the Kingdom of Heaven.

My dad, mother and brother Jesse were faithful, serving God to the end, and my brothers and I are still serving God, over forty years now, because we're thankful to Him for the saving and healing grace He has done in our lives.

I don't want to leave out what God did when He saved my brother Jesse from a near-death experience. At the time, we were temporarily living in Dodson, Texas, before we headed north as migrant workers. This was around 1960, and close to Christmas . Mom told us to go to church. It was John, Jesse and me. John was eleven, Jesse was eight, and I was six years old. When we arrived at church, there were only a few people there and we sat in the middle row. There was an elderly man singing a song and John was making us laugh on account of the man's singing. Thank God, they didn't kick us out. After the service, the people there gave us bags of treats to take home. As we were walking home from church, a young man about fourteen years old, driving a big truck, stopped and asked us if we wanted a ride. We said yes and climbed up on the back of the truck.

While Jesse was climbing, the driver took off at a high rate of speed. While John was trying to help Jesse get on, Jesse lost his grip and went down on the paved road. When the driver found out what happened, he stopped the truck and we got off and ran toward Jesse . The driver got scared and drove off. When we got to Jesse, he was crying and had a bloody face. It didn't look good.

Jesse asked John, "How do I look, *Manitu* ?" which is Spanish for "little brother."

John replied, "You look bad, you can see the bones in your face." This made Jesse cry even louder.

I felt sorry for him and said, "It's not all that bad, Manitu ," trying to encourage him.

A lady who was on the porch of her house and saw this came running and wrapped a towel around my brother's head. Jesse was taken to the doctor and sent home. We never found out what happened to the boy who was driving the truck. Eventually, Jesse got healed with no scars on his face. Jesse was the best-looking of us boys.

I remember around 1965, when we first arrived in Clinton, I was enrolled at Washington Elementary School. I had a lot of friends in school, probably because I was the only Mexican-American student at the time. I was in the fourth grade and Jesse was later enrolled in the same school and same grade I was in. W hen Jesse arrived in school, it seemed like I became transparent, because now all the students ignored me and wanted to be Jesse's friend. This made me kind of jealous of him. But eventually I got used to it. I guessed that's part of growing up.

Chapter IX

MORE MIRACLES

N ow I would like to tell you of other miracles which happen with the family of my sister-in-law, Elizabeth, or Beth, who married my brother, John.

Reverend Ernesto and Sister Maria Chapa had nine children, six boys and three girls. Reverend Chapa was an old-time Pentecostal preacher, who preached with authority. He once told me back in the old days, when he started preaching, there were no microphones, and preachers had to preach loud so all the people in the church could hear.

In this chapter, I would like to tell about some miracles God did in him, his family and friends. He once told me that all nine of their children were alive today because of a miracle God did in them. I'll start with the miracle God did in him.

When Brother Chapa married Sister Chapa, neither were born again Christians. Mr. Chapa was a gifted guitar player, who played his twelve-string guitar in beer joints and for Spanish dances. But he had a problem with seizures. He was a drinker and ready to fight if he was challenged. But he couldn't hold a steady job because of his seizures. When he had them, he fell on the ground.

Maria, the young girl he would meet one day, went to a Pentecostal church with her parents. She was not saved yet. Brother Chapa told me, one day, something happened that made his life turn around. After he married Sister Chapa and they were beginning to have children, she had gone to visit family with their children, and he was alone at home. After looking over his situation, not being able to hold down a steady job to support his family because of his epileptic seizures, he called upon God for help. He told God if He would heal him of this disease, he would give his life to Him, and if it was God's will, he would one day preach His Word. The Lord heard and answered his prayer by saving and healing him of that sickness.

After he prayed, Brother Chapa took the bottles of medications and threw them in the outhouse. That's what I call faith, believing God at His Word. The Lord, in Mark 11:24, said, "Therefore, I say unto you, whatever things ye desire, when ye pray, believe that ye receive them, and ye shall have them." (NSRB). After Sister Chapa returned home, Brother Chapa told her about the prayer he had made to God and that he threw out all his medications.

Sister Chapa said, "Are you crazy?"

But after she saw how God had healed and transformed the life of Brother Chapa, she, too, accepted the Lord as her personal Savior.

When Brother Chapa and Sister Chapa moved to Clinton to take over the church we were renting on North Second and Prairie Chief Avenue, the church building needed a lot of repairing. It had been vacant for some years. During this time that I helped Brother Chapa work on the church, he told me about how God had done many wonderful things in him and his family. He even told about how God brought back to life a young boy, who had drowned while swimming in a pond.

During this time, I learned many things from Brother Chapa. He taught me the Christian ministry, or I should say, how a minister sometimes goes through suffering . There were times when he was the pastor he had to walk to church on a dirt road, and a member of the church would pass by in his car and not pick him up. There were times he was accused of something wrong, and even though it wasn't true, he took the blame anyway, to keep new believers from a falling away, or quit serving God. There were times when he and Sister Chapa went hungry, so their children would not suffer hunger.

The reward for staying faithful to God outweighs all the suffering. As I said before, Brother Chapa once told me that all his children were alive today because of a miracle God had done.

For instance, there was the time when his three older boys were young and were driving on a county road, closed to Blair, Oklahoma. They had come to a stop sign and were ready to enter the main highway. As they were getting on the road, another vehicle drove right into them and the pickup his boys were in was totaled. All of his boys came out alive. Now, in those days, people drove between 55 and 65 mph, on the highway.

There was also the time his family was picking cotton, and two of his boys were on a tractor in the field . One was in the driver's seat and one was sitting by the wheel of the tractor. I don't know if the tractor was running or if one of them started it. One of the workers ran toward the tractor to try to stop it, but it was too late. The boy sitting by the wheel fell down and was run over by the tractor. That boy also came out from that accident without any broken bones.

I remember as a young boy, my parents and older siblings also worked picking cotton. There was a wooden trailer on the field, which was pulled by a tractor. For the new generation that never saw people picking cotton in the field , let me explain. When picking cotton by hand, the pickers would put the cotton in long sacks hanging from the shoulder, and would drag this sack until it got full. Some of these sacks were between five and twelve feet long. After the sack was full of cotton, they would weigh it, then pull it up to the trailer and empty the sack, then repeat the process. After the trailer was filled, a tractor would come to take it away and leave an empty trailer to get filled again. Well, one of Brother Chapa's boys got run over by one of these trailers, and again, no broken bones. Praise the Lord!

Now, let's return to the story of the boy who came back to life after he drowned in a pond . This happened not far from the town of Hobart, Oklahoma. Brother Chapa, his family and members of his church were visiting a family in a house outside of town, and there was a pond not far from the house. The older folks were having dinner outside when a boy came running, saying a boy named Rogelio, who was swimming in the pond, had gone under water and failed to come up. Now Rogelio was the son of Baldemar Hernandez. He and his family had begun going to Brother Chapa's church. When the men heard the bad news, they ran to the pond. Mr. Hernandez jumped into the water to join other boys, who were already searching for Rogelio.

Mr. Hernandez later testified that he said a prayer asking God, if his son was already gone, to help them at least find the body. Then Daniel , one of Brother Chapa's boys, saw the boy's body come up to the surface in front of him, got hold of the body and took it to the boy's father, who was already out of the water.

Then Brother Chapa said, "Give the boy to me."

I don't know what Brother Chapa said in that prayer, because I wasn't there, but God heard his prayer and brought that boy back to life, Praise God! Many years later, I heard Mr. Hernandez preach, and he sa id how God had brought his son back to life after he had drowned.

CHAPTER X

TIME SPENT LIVING IN CLINTON

From 1974 through 1979, as stated before, we lived in Clinton in the winter and spent summers living and working in Minnesota. In 1974, the year my brother, John, married Elizabeth, I graduated from Clinton High School. Something unusual happened in our graduation ceremony. We had a streaker in the auditorium, which is called the Tornado Dome. There must have been over 800 people in attendance when the streaker raced in front of all the people. He just wore a ski mask and tennis shoes. I, myself, didn't see him because our grad-uating class were sitting in the center of the building. I later found out the streaker was caught and suspended from school temporarily.

1974 was also the year I turned twenty years old. I was turning a new chapter in my life. The next four years, my life was made of working on a steady job, going to the pool hall downtown, and occasionally drinking beer with my friends. I never had a steady girlfriend during this time, even though I did go out with a native girl. She was about sixteen and I was twenty-three years old. We usually met at the pool hall and three or four girls were always with her. I had a friend whose name was Gilbert Rogue, who rode around in my car. Most of the time, we invited these girls to go with us and they did. I bought beer and wound up drinking out in the country. After drinking a few beers, this native girl and I would usually end up kissing, and that was all we did. This went on for about three months, then it was time for my family and me to go to Minnesota to work. After six months, we came back to Clinton and I still saw her at the pool hall, but there was no spark there anymore.

M y brother, Rudy, got married around 1980. My youngest brother, Robert, also got married around 1982. So, that left Mom and me living at home. Now, all four brothers had married and I still didn't have a girlfriend.

The good part was that I got saved in 1978, and Mom and I were doing the Lord's work during this time and for many more years. In 1984, Mom and I started a church in Clinton, and because of Mom's declining health, around 1989 we asked Rev. Ernesto Chapa to come to Clinton to take charge of the church . Thank God, he did. We really had a lot of respect for Brother Chapa, because he truly was a man used by God.

The same year, I met a young Christian woman who had been married, but now divorced. We dated for about five months and it seemed like she was the one God had brought into my life to marry. But when we made plans to get married, her parents didn't approve of us getting married. So, she and I prayed and fasted for God's will to be made clear. We didn't get married, and she later met and married another Christian man and they had three children. Today, they're no longer together.

Going back in time, in 1981, I started working at a plant called Collins and Aikman , where carpets were shaped to fit into new cars. I was hired as a night shift supervisor. I was in training while working for three months, then I worked for another three months. I got called to work at the U.S. Post Office as a clerk/letter-carrier.

While working at Collins/Aikman, I got to witness about God to some people who worked there. I remembered one man I witnessed to, whom I'll call LP. I already knew him because we both worked at Acme Brick Plant before it closed.

Anyway, I presented to him the plan of salvation that God has for everyone. Before I finished talking to him, I asked him, "What are you going to tell God on the Day of Judgement if you don't accept the Lord Jesus as your personal Savior?" He bowed his head, as if thinking what he was going to say. Then, with a smile, he said, "I'll ask Him if He wants to smoke a joint." Of course, he was being sarcastic. But again, that was how he was since I'd known him. He was always making jokes about everything. Back when my brothers, John and Jesse and I worked at Acme Brick Plant, he worked there too. Back then, my brothers and I weren't Christians, and we LP got along with him pretty well. Now, he couldn't understand that God had changed me and I was a new man with a different attitude and a new perspective on life. A joint, in this case, is dried marijuana leaves rolled up in thin paper to make a marijuana cigarette.

Another time, some Christian brothers and I went to LP's house to talk to him about God. There were about five of us in the group and LP knew all of us. Some had been his drinking "buddies" and John was with us, too. When we got there, I walked up to his house and John was a little distance behind me. I knocked at the door and LP opened the door.

When he saw me carrying a Bible, he said, "Are you coming again with that 'dung '?" By this time, he saw John walking up to the door and he started joking with him. He told John, "We're all sinners and are going to hell."

John responded, "I'm not, because I've accepted Jesus Christ as my personal Savior."

LP had a brother I'll call JP, who was the same age as John, and they both went to take the physical examination for the selective service in 1967, during the war in Vietnam. Both wanted to pass the exam and go together to fight the war. As fate would have it, John failed the exam because of flat feet, but JP passed, and after basic training was sent to Vietnam.

After we talked to LP for about five minutes, I gave him a tract and invited him to church, but he never went. I think that was the last time I saw LP. Many years later, JP saw John in a store and told him that he thought LP was dead because his family couldn't find him anywhere. He said he thought LP was killed by his own son and LP's own family buried him somewhere, because no body was ever recovered. JP was crying when he told John this.

You see, God is the righteous God and gives people the opportunity to know Him before they pass from this life to the next. 2 Peter 3:9 says, "...but is longsuffering towards us, not willing that any should perish, but that all should come to repentance." I thank God that today, I'm a child of the Living God and walking in newness of life, according to His Word. 2 Corinthians 5:17, "...old things have passed away, behold all things have become new."

While working at the Collins/Aikman plant, my job as night shift supervisor was to see that workers had plenty of carpets on hand so the work would not stop. There was a man there who drove a forklift, to bring the carpets on a pallet to the workers who ran the pressing machines. Whenever I told the man to bring more carpets, he would get mad and drive the forklift really fast, bringing the carpets and dropping the pallets really hard on the floor. One day, I talked to my boss and told him about him, but he said not to worry about him because that was the way he was. This made me feel uneasy.

Thank God I had a mother who knew how to reach Heaven with her prayers. Like I said before, Mom was a prayer warrior. One day, I told her about the man at work who didn't like me giving him orders. She told me not to worry. She was going to go before God with the petition and God was going to take care of it. The next day, I went to work. I told the man to bring more pallets and he did so without complaining.

And in a friendly mood, he even asked me, "Is there anything else you want me to do?"

Wow! Talk about God moving in a supernatural way. That forklift driver never gave me any more problems after Mom prayed. Praise God!

CHAPTER XI

GOD'S GOODNESS IS FOREVER

I started working at the Clinton U.S. Post Office in mid-November 1981, as stated before. I went on to work there for thirty-nine years and one-and-one-half month. I retired on December 31, 2020.

In my life time, I've seen God's hand working on me and my family, many times. I believe God's goodness and mercy are from everlasting to everlasting for His people, according to Isaiah 54:8, "In a little wrath I hid my face from thee for a moment, but with everlasting kindness will I have mercy on thee, saith the Lord, thy redeemer."

Working for the U.S. Post Office as a city letter carrier involves a lot of responsibility. You can't be daydreaming while delivering the mail, for it takes just a second to make a mistake. To me, a letter carrier is like an athlete who needs to be diligent, mentally and physically, able to do the job well. In the Clinton Post

Office, I saw two women try out for the city route job. One lasted half a day and the other lasted one day. I'm not saying women can't do this job, because when I retired there were more women working than men. A regular letter carrier has between 600 and 900 deliveries to make per day, in a timely manner. I thank God for giving me the strength and the wisdom to do my job well for all the years I worked there.

Every morning, before I go to work, I do my daily devotionals, to prepare myself not just mentally but spiritually. You see, putting God first is as important as breathing God's air. The same way we need food and water to keep our physical bodies functioning, we as Christians need God's Word and prayer to continue our walk with God.

I believe God blesses us every day. But to be blessed, we must live in obedience to His Word. Genesis 12:2,4 reads, "And I will make of thee a great nation and I will bless thee, and make thy name great, and thou shall be a blessing... So, Abram departed, as the Lord had spoken unto him..." But, sometimes, the devil, our enemy will try to rob us of God's blessings. John 10:10 says, "the thief has come to rob, to kill and destroy..." The thief here is the devil. His job is to rob us of God's blessing, and he also wants to kill us. But thank God, He is on our side. The devil can't do anything unless he has God's permission.

You see, this is a spiritual battle we Christians are fighting. A good example is Job in the Bible. Job was a rich man. He had many domestic animals , male and female servants, and was blessed with ten children. But there was a debate between God and the devil in Heaven. The devil told God that the only reason Job served the Lord was because God had blessed him with many riches and good health.

Then the devil said, "But put forth thine hand now, and touch all that he hath, and he will curse thee to thy face." God gave the devil permission to take away everything from Job. Even Job's wife told him to curse God and die. (Job 2:9) But the Bible says Job never cursed God, for he was faithful to God until the end of his trial. At the end, God blessed Job by giving him double of what he had before.

When God gave the Israelites the Promised Land of Canaan, the Israelites had to destroy the people living there to cleanse the land of idolatry. According to Exodus, Numbers, and Deuteronomy, it was a land flowing with many rich, natural resources, or "flowing with milk and honey," as the Bible calls it. But even though God gave them the land, "blessing" the Israelites, they had to fight for it. This was for the same reason God allowed the Aztecs, in Mexico, to be defeated by the Spanish conquistadors. Now, those who have studied history know the Aztecs were well advanced in civilization, but were into human sacrifice. Like some

Canaanites were idolaters and sacrificed their children to their god, Moloch . (2 Kgs 23:10)

Also, when the Europeans came to America, the land was in spiritual darkness. Many Europeans who came here were God-fearing people who brought Christianity to America.

I thank God that I was born in this country, where we have the freedom to preach and hear the gospel of our Lord and Savior, the Lord Jesus Christ. But sad to say, America has forgotten the roots this nation was founded upon. The Founding Fathers of this nation put God first in the laws and in the Constitution in our land. Today, people in high places of society are trying to erase God from the public or society. Many people have forgotten our nation is great because of the God-fearing people who lived before us. Psalm 33:12, says, "Blessed is the nation whose God is the Lord, and the people whom He hath chosen for His own inheritance." God forbid this nation will be like China, where God is the enemy of the country. If this ever happens, America will cease to be. I considered myself blessed to work with the U.S. Postal Service, but the devil tried to rob me of this blessing.

During the time when the Postal Service was financially unstable, when mail volume had gone to an all-time low because the computer age had taken over and people were not using the first-class mail to do business, jobs within the Postal Service were being eliminated and city routes were being added on, making them longer and eliminating some. Postal managers were sent to different towns to make city route adjustments. Our Post Office was no exception. My route added an hour of delivery and I was expected to make or finish it in eight hours. Our letter carrier union advised the letter carriers not to skip our ten-minute breaks or shorten our lunch breaks, and not to run on our routes, but to deliver our mail in a timely manner.

The Clinton Post Office was under new management and I was not making my route in eight hours the way management expected me to. So, the postmaster sent two supervisors to check on me to see if I was slacking on the job. This made me feel uneasy and uncomfortable. One day, while checking on me inside the post office, a supervisor told me I needed to think about my family, meaning I could lose my job if I didn't meet their expectations. Our letter carrier union steward heard him say that to me and later told me that if I wanted to file a grievance, he was there to help me. For some reason I never did, even though I had grounds to do so. In the Post Office, there is a rule that no employee should come to work feeling uneasy or under pressure due to harassment at work, either by management or a fellow employee.

But thank God, He came to my rescue again. I told Mom about it and we both prayed, and God took care of the problem, like in times past.

This problem went on for about two weeks, and being summer, I felt relieved because it was time for me to go on vacation. My vacation was for two weeks. When it was time to go back to work, I felt a little uneasy, expecting to continue where I left off. When I got to work, I found out the postmaster was gone and one of the supervisors who had followed me on my route was also gone. They had been sent to other post offices, I believe the ones they came from. The one supervisor still there had a change of heart, for he treated me really nice and worked with me to get my route back to where I could make it in eight hours. Thanks be to God! This happened around 2007, and the management I had when I retired were people who helped the postal employees feel they were working in a comfortable environment.

You see, Christians, we are not exempt from going through problems, but we have the Lord to help us go through them and give us courage to go through them. The problem may not go away right then, but He will give us the wisdom to follow through. Psalm 34:4,6 reads, "I sought the Lord, and He heard me, and delivered me from all my fears.... This poor man cried, and the Lord heard him, and saved him out of all his troubles." Psalm 46:1, "God is our refuge and strength, a very present help in trouble." Psalm 121:8, "The Lord shall preserve thy going out and thy coming in from this time forth, and for everlasting."

Someone might say, "It's all pure luck, why make a big deal out of it?" Well, I'm going to say what a black brother by the name of Tyone Lewis once told me . He didn't believe in good luck. He said, "It's either a blessing or a curse." He was right, because the Bible doesn't mention the word "luck."

As a man of God, I see the Lord's blessings all around me, every day. For example, in the last two months I've been retired from work. I haven't received my retirement pay yet, and yet God has helped me, because all my bills have been paid and I don't lack anything. I've already talked to the place that's supposed to send the retirement payment, and they told me it has been sent already. Another blessing came just last week. I was told I would be receiving benefits that some people told me I wasn't going to get . Yesterday, I received a lump sum amount for five months I should have been paid for, and didn't.

This reminds me of Psalm 37:25, "I have been young and now I am old, yet have I not seen the righteous forsaken, nor his seed begging bread." You see, God's blessing doesn't just come because we're Christians, but they come if we're doing what He tells us to do. Obedience is the key word here. For instance, a Christian who doesn't pay his tithes and offerings to carry on God's work shouldn't expect His blessings.

I might be stepping on some toes here, but I've got to speak the truth, as God gives it to me. I don't like to beat around the bush, as we sometimes say. In my life time, I've seen Christians having difficulty paying their bills and going around borrowing money, for this same reason. We read about this in Malachi 3:8-12. It says there, God's people can rob God when we don't pay our tithes and offerings, and we are cursed with a curse. But we are blessed abundantly when we obey. In 2 Corinthians 9:7, it says, "Every man according as he purposeth in his heart, so let him give, not grudgingly, or of necessity, for God loveth a cheerful giver." Not too long ago, a brother from the church was trying to convince me we don't have to give our tithes and offerings to be blessed. He even asked another minister who was present, and the minister told him, "You can't be blessed if you don't give your tithes and offerings to the Lord." It's all there in God's Word, in black and white, but at times people try to have an excuse to not have to give.

During my lifetime as a Christian, which is more than forty-two years, I've had the privilege of meeting many brothers and sisters who have been a blessing in my life and my family's lives. Even though there have been many, I will now mention one, because he was instrumental in buying our church, which we really needed. His name is brother Willie Flores . I believe God brought this brother to us for a special reason. As stated earlier in the book , we started having services in our house, back in the last part of 1984. Including Mom and me, there were about eight of us who gathered with Rev. Ernesto Chapa and his wife, coming from Hobart, and Rev. Chapa would play his bass guitar.

The following year, we rented an old library building in the town of Arapaho. We were here for about four years. Back then, it was called, The Spanish Mission. It was here that brother Willie and his family started coming to our services. Mom, being the pastor, gave him a part in bringing God's Word. From there, we went back to Clinton, and rented a small church. We were there for about two years. This church had been the Church of the First Born but it had closed. Then, after two years, the owner told us we needed to look for another building, because they were going to use the church again. So, we started looking for a church to rent. This was around 1987. With God's help, we found the church building where we are presently at, on 201 Prairie Chief Avenue. Here the name was changed to Templo Maranatha. Templo meaning "temple" in Spanish and Maranatha, which is an Aramaic word, meaning "Our Lord Cometh," in reference to Jesus' coming. An event that every born again Christian looks forward to.

The Church of God organization owned this building. We started paying rent. I think we were blessed to be in this building. It had a sanctuary, which held around 100 people, an office, two classrooms, two bathrooms, a large diner and a kitchen. The parsonage was located in the back of the church building.

After two years paying rent, we decided we wanted to buy the church, even though we didn't have the money to do so. We were acting by faith. We asked how much they were asking for the church and the property, if they were to sell it. They said $20,000. Now that was a great blessing, because that church was worth a lot more, like $85,000 . Our church bank account was between $2,000 and $3,000 . When we asked for a loan of $20,000, it was denied. So, it was time for us to bow the knee and go before God in prayer. After some time praying, God heard our prayers. No, He didn't send a check for $20,000, but He gave Brother Willie a plan to buy the church, in a dream.

This was the plan : There were six brothers in the church who had income. If each of these brothers gave $120 a month as payments toward buying the building, that would be $720 per month, and in two-and-a-half years, the church would be paid for. After hearing the plan, we were delighted! We were all gung-ho and were eager to start. What we didn't know was that old split-foot, the devil himself, had plans to keep us from buying the church. He attacked us financially. And as any minister of God knows, any time God's people start doing something for the glory of God, the enemy will attack to keep us from doing the Lord's will.

Not long after we started making the church payments, a brother got laid off, another one left the church, and a third brother got his hours shortened at work. So, that left three of us with the load. But I'm always amazed how God has a backup plan when it involves His Kingdom. I've heard it said in the past, and I'll repeat it : "If there is a will, there's a way, and if you believe God and move forward, He will make a way for you." Back then, I was the treasurer of the church, and my job was to send the monthly payments of $720 to buy the church. So, the three of us making the monthly payments of $120 came to $360 . We were still short $360 to make the $720 payment. So, I had to take the money from the church account to come up with the $720.

Here is the divine intervention. For a long time, I did this and the church account never went down. It seemed to stay in the same amount every month, whenever I got the bank statement. And on top of that, I was paying the utility bills from this account. Praise God! Periodically, the sisters of the church made bake sales to help out, but it wasn't a whole lot. Later, Brother Willie, whose hours were shortened, got a second job to help out with the payments.

This reminds me of the story in 1 Kings 17:8-16, where God sent Elijah to a widow to be fed by her during a time of hunger, for it had not rained for a long time and there were no crops. Now, this widow just had enough food for her and her son to eat their last meal and then die of hunger. But the prophet told her to make him a small cake for him and they could eat the rest. He told them God had said the barrel of meal and the cruse of oil would not run empty until the rain came. In verse 15, it says, "she went and did according to the saying of the prophet." That's how faith works, obeying God even though your mind doesn't comprehend it.

Hebrews 11:1 says, "Now, faith is the substance of things hoped for, the evidence of things not seen." Amen. Now, we could have easily given up when those three brothers couldn't make those payment and said, "We tried, but it didn't work." But there wouldn't be any glory given to God in this case. In two-and-a-half years, the church was paid for in full. Thank You, Jesus.

Month later, my brother, John, got a job and helped finish paying for the church. We started with six brothers and ended with six. Who were they? Well, it was Rev. Ernesto Chapa, me, David Martinez, Willie Flores, John and the Lord Jesus Christ. Hallelujah!!

IN CONCLUSION

T oday, or should I say, to this day, the church is still here. People have come and some have moved on to other churches, but we sing a song in Spanish that says, "Even through trials, the church keeps moving forward, it just stops to preach (God's Word) ." Some brethren who were a blessing to the church are with the Lord now. For instance, Rev. Ernesto and Maria Chapa, Licensed Minister Catarina Rivera (Mom) and Jesse, my brother. I'm sure they're looking down from Heaven and telling us to continue doing God's will. I really miss them, and can't wait to be with them one day.

I hope what I said in this book will be as much a blessing to you as it was to me. The reasons that le d me to write this book are that my mother's legacy will not be forgotten, and to remind people that the Lord Jesus is the miracle worker and, "He is still the Miracle Worker."